Porcelain

Poem on the Downfall of My City

DURS GRÜNBEIN

TRANSLATED BY KAREN LEEDER

LONDON NEW YORK CALCUTTA

This publication was supported by a grant from
the Goethe-Institut, India.

Seagull Books, 2020

Originally published as *Porzellan: Poem vom Untergang meiner Stadt*
by Durs Grünbein, 2005

© Suhrkamp Verlag, Frankfurt am Main, 2005

All rights reserved by and controlled through Suhrkamp Verlag Berlin

First published in English translation by Seagull Books, 2020

English translation © Karen Leeder, 2020

*Except for Figure 7, images are taken from a private collection of
postcards in the author's possession*

*Figure 7 © Kupferstich-Kabinett, Staatliche Kunstsammlungen Dresden.
Photograph by Herbert Boswank.*

ISBN   978 0 8574 2 781 6

British Library Cataloguing-in-Publication Data
A catalogue record for this book is available from the British Library

Typeset by Seagull Books, Calcutta, India
Printed and bound by Hyam Enterprises, Calcutta, India

Contents

vii

'Of Things Broken and Lost'
Durs Grünbein's Dresden

Karen Leeder

1

Porcelain
Poem on the Downfall of My City

62

A Glossary

69

Notes

92

Translator's Acknowledgements

'Of Things Broken and Lost'
Durs Grünbein's Dresden

The bombing of Dresden on the night of 13–15 February 1945 by American and British planes (75 years ago this year) is one of the most controversial military acts of the Second World War. First, the deliberate practice of area bombing, designed to cause chaos in a city known to house many refugees, the particulars of the raids (the repeated sorties and their scale), and the tactics employed meant that this was seen as an unprecedented attack on a defenceless city. In fact, other Allied raids were more ferocious in many ways but this particular target acquired a special significance: Dresden was styled as a city of culture, a symbol of German identity. The silhouette of Dresden as a Baroque Florence on the Elbe immortalized by the Italian landscape artist Canaletto eclipsed its role as centre of industry, garrison city and communications hub.

This victim-narrative was, crucially, taken up into the official line in the GDR (East Germany) after the war, which saw the attacks on Dresden as the ultimate symbol of imperialist aggression, formally dubbed 'the Anglo-American Terror-Bombing', after a phrase concocted by the Nazi Minister of Propaganda, Joseph Goebbels. In the West too, during the 1980s, the popularity of accounts, like those of David Irving exaggerating the death toll and comparing the act to the Holocaust, continued to contribute to the sense that the destruction of Dresden was a unique and symbolic act.

It is no surprise therefore that after the unification of Germany, Dresden became the icon of German suffering in the Second World War. In part this symbolic value allowed the destruction of the city to become understood as a violation not only of the city itself but of German culture per se. Family stories of the devastation began to emerge, along with other victim narratives, the sinking of the Wilhelm Gustloff (memorably recounted in Günter Grass's 2002 *Crabwalk*) or accounts of the mass rape of German women by the Red Army. However, when the writer W. G. Sebald, in his Zurich Lectures (*On the Natural History of Destruction*) in 1997, launched his influential thesis that German post-war literature had been criminally silent on such events, Dresden was already a glaring counter-example. Most of the literature on Dresden had been written by those who experienced the bombing first-hand, as adults or children—from the famous diaries of Victor Klemperer, for whom the bombing meant escape from almost certain death (as a Jew), to an international bestseller like Kurt Vonnegut's *Slaughterhouse-Five*, which recounted in part the author's experience as a prisoner of war in the city.

German writer Durs Grünbein, born in the Hellerau suburb of Dresden in 1962, had no direct experience of the bombing itself, but he grew up with the aftermath both in the ruins about him and within his own family. The first poem in *Porcelain* ironically foregrounds the 17 years that separate the events of February 1945 from his birth. Although some of the ruins were physically present in the Dresden of his youth (notably the statue of Luther he describes glaring fiercely down upon him), the destruction was more present in its absence: the areas of emptiness in the midst of the energetic East German rebuilding programme. These gaps symbolized the inaccessibility of the catastrophe, to be sure, but also served as a screen for nostalgic projections of the past among those coming to terms with it: the 'song of the Lorelei' of Poem 5. Indeed, Grünbein characterized his own response to the events so often recalled by his family as 'phantom pain'.

This book-length poem, with 49 rhymed 10-line strophes in classical metre is his most sustained and personal attempt to date to come to terms with the events of 1945. The long poem, or sequence or cycle (he refers to it differently in different places) began, he explains, as a ritual, a game even, in that he had sat down on the anniversary of the bombings each year between 1992 and 2005, and written a poem in the same form, which he had then gathered and expanded for publication.

The German title *Porzellan*, however, also carries within it a covert reference to the secret dedicatee of the work: Holocaust poet Paul Celan. Celan haunts the work in many senses: both explicitly within the mottos, for example, to Poem 25, but also in countless unmarked borrowings, some of the most important of which are mentioned in the notes.[1]

His presence also signals the aesthetic and political project of the work: to place the events of February 1945 within the larger context of German aggression during the War. This is part of Grünbein's argument against Dresden's stylization of itself as a victim removed from the logic of war, and indeed its broader sense of exceptionalism and victimhood during GDR days and beyond (see Poem 12).

The point goes to the heart of Dresden's continued self-understanding and Grünbein also courts controversy in the way he makes it. In Poem 4, for example, the destruction of Dresden porcelain as the Allied bombers approach is linked to the violence inflicted on the Jewish population during the war. The sound of the porcelain segues into the smashing glass of *Kristallnacht,* almost like a film dissolve, making a political point—about Dresden's demise being the ultimate consequence of Nazi Germany's actions—in symbolic terms. But the poem betrays unease in the juxtaposition even as it draws it. The movement between the November pogroms of 1938 and Ash Wednesday bombing of 1945 is 'nur ein Sprung' in German. But this is not so much 'just a hop skip and a jump' or 'leap' (one meaning of this fatefully overdetermined word) as an uncomfortable rupture of tone, here also embedded in the 'Narrensprung', the carnival dance performed as part of the culturally sanctioned overturning of orders. A 'Sprung', after all, is also a crack in the porcelain itself.

But the city's fate is also placed in a wider historical context and the poem goes back to the founding of the baroque pearl on the Elbe, dwelling on the Saxon court of Augustus the Strong (1670–1733), and the founding of the Meissen pottery in the eighteenth century that brought Dresden its wealth, through the war, the bombing, the GDR years (1949–90) and the reconstruction of the Frauenkirche (Church of Our Lady) in 2004. On the way, it cites a whole gamut of literature, art and music dedicated to the city, including the works by Klemperer and Vonnegut mentioned above along with a host of modern European work.

Although the poem has itself been turned into a libretto, performed in the Frauenkirche on the anniversary of the bombings, and has also appeared in a limited edition with illustrations by Ralf Kerbach, the critical response in reviews and academic articles has been mixed. Certain aspects of this response are fascinating in themselves: misreadings or partial readings (perhaps fuelled by the lack of notes in the German edition) that turn crucially on the issue of perspective. But many of these critics were also writing at a time only shortly after unification, when Dresden was in the centre of a cultural war about the legitimacy of German mourning—a discussion that continues to this day, sharpened by the political propaganda of the new right. In February 2020, in an article in *Der Spiegel* titled 'The Misused Tragedy', Grünbein deplored how mourning for the destroyed city had been instrumentalized by the political right, thus obscuring with their revisionist politics the right of ordinary people to mourn. So, Grünbein's is also a political intervention: allowing Dresden's fate to be reinserted into the narrative which gave rise to it, placing it within different historical trajectories and perspectives.

More than anything, as I have discovered talking about this work to audiences in Germany, UK and the US, it is clear what an emotional charge this subject retains for many, how it lives on in families, and how curiously visceral the responses are to a work attempting to approach this legacy. This anniversary edition includes notes, both Grünbein's own, in which he addresses some of the criticisms for the first time, and others to aid those reading in an English-language context. It also includes new illustrations and a new poem written especially for the publication. It is also, of course, in English—which will, it is hoped, allow the concerns of the poem (thematic and aesthetic) to emerge more clearly from out of the political debates without getting caught immediately in the fraught arena of the German-language context.

A central issue for the critics was the very fact of someone born after, the prominent 'Johnny-come-lately' of the poem, writing about what he had not experienced himself. On the one hand, Grünbein was criticized for not doing justice to the horror, because he remained too distanced and without emotion, too cynical. At the same time, his supposed evocation of distance sat uncomfortably with the real biographical details of his own family: his mother's survival as a child. On the other hand, he was also seen as an intruder, taking possession of suffering that was not rightfully his, usurping others' experience. This work then raised in an acute form the very legitimacy of post-memorial writing per se.

Related to this was a perceived unease at what was read as an uncertainty of tone in the poem, especially the juxtaposition, it was claimed, of a voyeuristic fascination with the violence of the events to an excessive pathos, particularly in the family stories, and kitsch in the fetishization of the porcelain. This tied in for many with discomfort over the sexualization of Dresden, a charge that became more pointed after a 2005 interview in which Grünbein called the poem a 'rape fantasy'.[2] Some also found the aesthetic form incongruous: from the highly rhetorical German 'Poem' of the title (implying classical grandeur) to the fact that the poem is rhymed and moves in and out of classical metre, shifting between high poetic diction, irony, humour and the downright demotic, concerned always with the poet's role as a keeper and creator of memories, 'changing places, times, dimensions as he goes—goes on—creating' (49). A review by Michael Braun (to which Grünbein returns in this edition) was tellingly entitled 'Is There a Language for the Inferno?' raising the stakes and self-consciously connecting the work to the post-1945 discussions inspired by Theodor W. Adorno about how to find a language adequate for the Holocaust.[3]

I mention these things here because they go to the heart of what the poem is about. For whatever reason, critics have too often missed the fact that the poem as a whole rehearses precisely these dilemmas as a way of questioning the very premise of who can write about such things and how. This is placed centre stage from the very beginning with the seemingly oblique reference to elegy returning as hiccups in the first poem, one of the many places where Celan is referenced. In his 'Deine Augen im Arm' ('Your Eyes embraced'), Celan's lyric subject attempts to swallow the ashes representing the genocide, but they return as 'Aschen-/Schluckauf' ('Ash-/hiccups'). Grünbein seems to be suggesting the same is still true. Indeed, his poem is an exploration of how to mourn and how the mourning of ordinary Germans has been distorted by the political agenda of the right.

What is more—and this should not really need stating—the lyric subject of the poem should not be confused with Grünbein himself. It is clear that many voices are overheard, spliced together and quoted here, not only poets and writers but also politicians, soldiers, historians, journalists, ordinary people, myths. Together they create a fragmented choral requiem rising over the ruins. In the same way, the poem often autocorrects, testing out different approaches, criticizing its own lapses in taste, as if trying out different ways of citing the different voices and creating forms of address. In the same spirit, the poem also thematizes looking and not looking, seeing and not seeing, as well as the explicit issue of perspective. Poem 32, for example, sees the silhouette of Dresden drawn in cavalier perspective; Poem 17 ironically employs the bird's-eye view of a sparrow sitting on the famous statue of the Golden Rider Augustus. Others make use of instruments: the child under museum lights with a magnifying glass, examining the famous Baroque cherry stone from the Green Vault carved with 185 heads screaming in horror; at yet another point it is the lens of a wedding snapper at a family wedding which gains a further charge from being seen through a subterranean reference to a poem by Philip Larkin; or, elsewhere, a brain scanner examining the cerebral cortex, as in Poem 20. Poem 22 offers a nightmare vision of a lone statue helplessly surveying the devastation, which seems to imply the famous photograph of Dresden taken by Richard Peter in 1945. That is to say that 'visions' of Dresden are being juxtaposed, examined and turned this way and that, looked at from multiple perspectives, just like the family heirlooms of Meissen porcelain in Poem 17.

For sure, there is an emotional attachment to the poet's hometown; but not to the point of ignoring its part in the logic of war. Even that attachment is challenged. Grünbein has repeatedly called the poem 'impossible troubadour poetry'. The city is 'the lost beloved in the distance' charged with 'secret eroticism'. Setting aside the fact that Grünbein's poetics are inevitably erotic in their encounter with the European tradition,[4] this trope reaches a climax in his interview already referred to which interprets the bombing of Dresden as a rape fantasy. But this is not Grünbein's fantasy. Instead, he cites it as part of a culturally legitimized fascination with the violation of beauty in art and literature (Dresden is seen through the lens of art throughout in this poem). But Grünbein also charts the terrible historical reality of such attitudes in the accounts of the pilots from the Gulf War (where the sexualization of bombing was ubiquitously documented) and projects those back onto those Allied bombers in 1945 following the sinuous 'S' of the Elbe towards their target (see Poem 2). And the feminization of the city also goes hand in hand with an alternative and very sympathetic depiction of the maternal. But the destruction is then reinterpreted, so as to move beyond the historical specificity and view the violation structurally, as it were. In his recent essay on the role of aerial photography in war, Grünbein pinpoints this again as an issue of perspective: 'the aerial view is the phantasm of false sovereignty'.[5]

Finally, any sense that the 'elegance' of Grünbein's poetry serves as an obscene decoration to the horrors it adumbrates is surely wrong. In fact, rhyme functions, as does the rhythm, as part of a highly self-conscious strategy both to suggest past glory, past wholeness, as well as to subvert it; that is to say, deliberately missed rhyme or half-rhyme signals the gap between wholeness and ruin, between pre- and post-war imaginings—between Goethe, say, and Celan. In Poem 49 Grünbein even acknowledges the 'heikle Formen' ('dicey forms') of the Dresden figurines, but also, clearly, his own poem. This is important. One of the inspirations for the poem that Grünbein cites in his new glossary is Czesław Miłosz: his 'Song of Porcelain' (Washington DC, 1947) which he claims was the initial inspiration for his work. Grünbein continues: '"Sir, Porcelain troubles me most" was the line that pierced my heart. The sad little cry of cups and saucers, cracked [. . .]. Verses on the destruction of these insignificant objects in modern wars, the crunch of broken pieces under the feet of the survivors, you never forget that' (see p. 65–6).

The line from Miłosz's 'Piosenka o porcelanie', written in American exile in 1947, is one of many shards of European poetry that trouble Grünbein's poem. The broken porcelain cups and saucers represent not only all that has been lost through the violence of war but also the legacy of what remains in many Dresdners' homes. Finally, also, as Geoffrey Hartman has noted of Miłosz, 'the inadequacy of those fragile symbols'. The failure of porcelain to carry the weight of history is heard in the broken, even pained, half-rhyme of the refrain ('pana' / 'porcelany'), brilliantly captured in Robert Hass's translation: 'Of all things broken and lost / Porcelain troubles me most'.[6]

Those lines are, for me, programmatic and one of the reasons I wanted to translate this work: Grünbein's poem attempts not to make the losses of Dresden whole but to capture the memory of wholeness and the reality of loss in the form itself. It might be tempting to think of his poetry as alchemy of a sort (especially given the attention Grünbein pays to court alchemist Johann Friedrich Böttger—'ducatshitter' and accidental inventor of Dresden's 'white gold'). But that would be too complete a transformation for what Grünbein performs. That is to say, the poem is not to be read as an undisturbed whole, nor seen to represent a single perspective. And here its composition history is illuminating. It is an aesthetic of 'short exposure times': the need, as Grünbein explains, 'to hold on to the moment in which the word is illuminated in a flash before it sinks back into the twilight of the general language usage' (see p. 67).

As luck would have it, an extraordinary synergy occurred as I was finishing work on these poems which presented me with a way of thinking about what he is doing. Writer, ceramicist and artist Edmund De Waal's 'Library of Exile' exhibition opened in February 2020 in the Japanishes Palais, Dresden (that is, the building that housed Augustus's Porcelain collection) and moved on to the British Museum, London. In it, among much else, he presents 18 plates bought at auction, part of the estate of the Jewish von Klemperer family, who fled from Dresden in 1938 and whose collection was confiscated and handed over to the Nazis. The plates suffered extensive damage during the bombing in 1945 and are cracked, broken and blackened with fire damage. De Waal, however, invited Japanese artist Maiko Tsutsumi to reassemble them using the traditional *kintsugi* method of mending with gold lacquer. *Kinstugi* is the ancient Japanese method of mending the cracked porcelain vessels for tea ceremonies, so that the mend is visible, and the object can be appreciated with all its history. The gold lacquer marks the moments of fracture, the moments in which something has been lost, and serves both to make apparent the fact of artistic dialogue and to place the object within a historical time span that goes beyond the life of the artist and the present of the object itself. Grünbein's *Porcelain*, then, as *kintsugi*? The shards of history still there as fragments, turned in the hands of the poet, looked at from every angle, but also worked with words, to make an object that bears its historical scars and speaks to its present.

Karen Leeder
Oxford, 2020

Notes

1   See, for example, Durs Grünbein in conversation with Michael
    Eskin, in Michael Eskin, *Schwerer werden. Leichter sein: Gespräche
    um Paul Celan* (Frankfurt: Suhrkamp, 2020), where the poet
    discusses his debt to Celan and Eskin mentions many of the
    references.

2   '"Cadences in the Gaps of Time": The Poet, the Past and *Porzellan*',
    in Michael Eskin, Karen Leeder and Chris Young (eds), *Durs
    Grünbein: A Companion* (Berlin and New York: de Gruyter, 2013),
    pp. 219–34.

3   Michael Braun, 'Gibt es eine Sprache für das Inferno? Ein Poem
    auf Dresdens Untergang von Durs Grünbein', *Neue Zürcher
    Zeitung*, 22 September 2005.

4   See Michael Eskin's wonderful comparative study: *Poetic Affairs:
    Celan, Grünbein, Brodsky* (Stanford, CA: Stanford University Press,
    2008).

5   Durs Grünbein, *Jenseits der Literatur: Oxford Lectures* (Frankfurt:
    Suhrkamp, 2020).

6   Czesław Miłosz, *Selected and Last Poems, 1931–2004* (Robert Hass
    trans.) (London: Penguin Classics, 2017).

Figure 1. Dresden before the destruction 1945, view from the West.

For my mother

'My little bird will not come'
Immanuel Kant, 1803

1

Why complain, Johnny-come-lately? Dresden was long gone
when your little light first appeared on the scene.
Moist eyes are not the same as grey hair, my son.
And, as your name suggests, you're too quick for it, too green.
Seventeen years, barely a childhood, was all it took
to erase what had been there before. The sombre grey
of uniformity had closed the wounds and magic ceded to—
bureaucracy. No need for them to slay the Saxon peacock.
Lichen blossomed on the sandstone flowers, implacably.
Why brood? It comes back like hiccups: elegy.

2

Frosty night air: below the wings a sight for weary eyes,
the river's slender S, beckoning the bombers on.
City with no time for dressing up that night.
Witch on a broomstick, brewing glass, metal, asphalt, stone.
Bomb after polished bomb, tumbling from the bay,
tons of rubble fall into the mistress's waiting lap.
'This night is irredeemable.' . . . Augustus's pride and joy—
bright sandstone castle—phosphorus burns it black.
The skies of Spain alight and Guernica and Coventry.
Of the bella *ante bellum*—nothing left to see.

3

Say after me: it doesn't take much to make
a moonscape of a city. Or charcoal of the folk
who lived there. Imagine this: in the time it takes
to nip out of the opera for a pack of fags
the streets were death traps, bubbling with tar.
Just now, frost, hands frozen blue on handlebars,
then the sea of houses was raked by desert winds.
Stiff as pharaohs in their winter coats they burned.
Never was a summer hotter. The last alarm
hardly faded—and the ashes were still warm.

'. . . 2,000 tons of the good porcelain clay'

Johann Friedrich Böttger, Alchemist of the Saxon Court

Porcelain, endless porcelain was ground to dust,
crockery, cups and figurines: whitest Meissen gold.
But not just that. *Ach, once upon a time*—the faintest
tinkling, then across the crime scene the thunder rolled.
Not a rowdy wedding-do. It was *The Night of Broken Glass*
or, what sharp-tongued folk called: the glazier's lucky day.
And Ash Wednesday just a hop, skip and jump away.
Fools and Nazis—huzzah!—sure, they had a blast.
What's that? Innocent? Disgrace came long ago.
Dresden shepherdesses, *German bands*, where are you now?

5

Every year in February it touches on a nerve,
that distant call of the Lorelei: *Dresden, Dresden . . .*
Silent film on late-night TV and there it is: archive
of the city as it was, unharmed: no consolation.
Off to watch the newsreels, passers-by, no idea what
was to come, flâneurs, stylish ladies, invalids.
There, in Postplatz: trams, a bicycle, horse and cart,
a cinematic world filled with Dietrichs, Buster Keatons.
Resplendent on the Altmarkt Square, only Germania
stands above the traffic like a diva straight from Wagner.

6

Let Dresden be. You won't find what you're looking for.
How vulgar—the invalid acting like she's deaf.
Only the body here to visit, an inspector.
When she was sad, mother's mother used to reminisce
about the city in the valley, in her beauty sleep, content.
No, memory, the store of myth is dry, those legends
long run out, your every homecoming hell-bent.
Only the old man at the Friedrichstor, with empty hands
doesn't need to look. Blind, he knows the shape, the form,
of every house—of all that vanished in the firestorm.

7

This marvellous thing, not even thumbnail-sized,
a stone spat out by a cherry thief—no more.
As a child I'd stare at it for hours, under museum lights
and magnifying glass, like a tiny planet seen from afar.
Carved in hard wood, a jeweller's masterpiece:
eyes wide with terror, on every tiny screaming face,
inferno on a needle tip; the droplets glisten.
Hard to fathom, there—*in nuce*—what would come to pass:
emblem of the future and my hometown Dresden
was itself that cherry pip as seen from outer space.

8

'. . . I did say yes
O at lightning and lashed rod . . .'

Gerard Manley Hopkins,
'The Wreck of the Deutschland'

Black snow. Here at the very start of childhood.
Dresden rests, a ruined city, proud and mute.
Elbe, lazy river—I was yours from the start.
I saw my parent's home engulfed in mud.
In winter when cupola and dome are white with snow,
the ravaged city fills my soul with shame, simply shame.
Rubens, Rembrandt, Raphael—then nothing more to show . . .
Your downfall is the stuff of trashy melodrama.
How long ago was that? Don't ask me, I can't say.
The only word I know for 'gone forever' is 'today'.

9

'That's why I sometimes close my eyes and think of Dresden—'

Heinrich von Kleist, 1801

City doomed to ruin: what a wretched turn of phrase.
Just a fig leaf for hubris, no? For blindness and bombast.
Does that mean that she deserved this grisly fate?
City giddy with her own beauty, this proud place?
Only Atlas, fountain nymph, relieved at last
of his sandstone burden, gets to say. The great
giant Rübezahl descended from the mountains out of love
for the dryad Elbe, club-wielding muscleman of lore.
These cupolas, cake moulds for the dough of clouds above,
dreamed on oblivious—as they lay broken on the floor.

Cool it, greenhorn. When that glory passed away,
you weren't even there. The things your mother saw,
scarcely five years old, you'll never read in her eyes. War,
trauma, these things are not carried in your DNA.
Block out those words you heard from childhood on:
the family sigh 'Poor city'. You stood there, the stolid one.
Dresden, Dresden, you know who left it high and dry:
not the Brits, and no, not Uncle Sam. It was your own crew
that gave up your birthright for a bowl of lentil stew.
Hurting still? City in the valley. Only a tourist would ask why.

11

Yes, it hurts. A bullet you can bite—but
never digest. And so, the old sense of shame
strikes up with the first bars of Mozart's *Magic Flute*.
That February night, clear as stars, comes back again.
It never will be done. And what the people hear in everything
—Papageno, Papagena stuttering—
is the echo of that triad, the same old refrain,
destruction. The hated theme hangs heavy in the air.
As for tragedy, no way! Where, if not here, were we
the 'Hans in Luck' of fairy tale? No flies on him.

12

'The Elbe disappeared upstream and downstream in the grey mist'

Carl Gustav Carus, 1814

Gobsmacked, eh? The tourist asks, can this be it?
Sister of Venice, Florence on the Elbe, this is Dresden?
This provincial dump, soviet triste, grey concrete?
Poor city. True, she can no longer hold her own
among the beauties spared by war. So how come,
even in a rage, she touches me like this? Everyone
laughs when the locals sing her praise in broadest Saxon.
Each of them a little prince cheated of his throne.
And nothing left for them—but a vivid imagination.
Genius loci, guess who does the restoration.

'And if any mischief follow, then
thou shalt give . . . burning for burning'

Exodus 21

No sweat, Arthur, you only did what you had to do.
A duel requires a steady hand, nerves of steel, it's true,
though *Blitzkrieg* is more Moses: an 'eye for an eye' kind of deal.
You knew your Bible back to front, had an iron will,
got 'em though, the Huns, Nibelungs—and Antichrists, why not.
No need to tell an Englishman about what's fair.
'Acts of terror'? Memo. Your canny Prime Minister—
washed his hands of it, like Pilate. Whiter than white,
he's gone down in history. Now the fat is in the fire:
Terror-Merchant, Bingo-Bomber, Desk-Pirate of the Skies.

14

Still not done? What about the seventeenth of April?
Alarms wake those still left among the ruins, the bereaved.
Spring, a shadow of life. Out of nowhere, into the still
of the graveyard, bursts a squadron of killer bees.
Flying Fortress is the scourge, takes the time it likes.
All quiet below, apathy, no flak-guns thunder.
Forests, motorways—just a field of rubble. 'Alright!'
And just like that the world we knew went under,
Dresden now was just a patch of prairie land.
....
Him come from the future, *ex machina*, forgive the man.

15

After the completed renovation
of the Frauenkirche, 23 June 2004

Our memory a pendulum . . . then and now . . .
always swinging back and forth. Tread carefully, though
it will curtail your little span and, slowing, take its toll.
You're struck when you hear how she came to fall,
only later, after the night of bombs had passed.
Frauenkirche, gracious one, gave her children time
to heal. Though sorely wounded, held out to the last,
standing proud, despite her broken spine.
After and before. . . . Her subsidence the caesura.
All those years the lesson was: stay upright just like her.

16

Luther standing there: the image that I can't let go.
Surrounded by a wasteland, shoots of tender green,
under a disdainful sky, almost forgotten, *memento*
of the blaze: and in this urban desert, a window arch remains.
Do you recall? The lonely risalit, black with soot,
moaning soundlessly, like the *o* in torso . . . chorus . . . baroque.
A mote like this in your eye and you're stuck
with it for life. And yet the greatest shock
was not the ruined church, his final thesis—
but that all around the sheep grazed on oblivious.

This inscription in the Dresden valley is the very last
thing to be lost. Hogarth's flourish lives on in the chronicle
and echoes down the centuries like the name Assurbanipal.
Oh Lord . . . What? The unspeakable. Here it came to pass.
Picture Venus, ventured deep into the land of mist
looking for a place of refuge as she's chased through
Europe, now transforms herself—into porcelain.
The emblem of crossed swords is known to be the sign.
Precious heirlooms brought out at every family do.
Plates and cups turned endlessly that way and this.

Elbe-valley, seven bridges, you can see them in your dreams.
Bet you can trace the city's every contour in your sleep?
Like Polyphemus in his cave once knew his sheep.
Like the astronomer who loves his favourite constellation,
from Hellerau to Cotta you know every property.
The blindfold kid will always find the penguins in Dresden zoo.
They say good luck lives on in families. Well, misfortune too.
Shut your eyes and ruins are the first thing that you see
burnt into your retina, even after forty years.
Familiar as the lines upon your hand, the city map appears.

Figure 2. The Elbe, iced over, in 1929.

19

Time to sleep. Every night the magic word
as mother tucked you in, it was the final chord
of the final lullaby. No point then to if or but.
That was it: the book of fairy tales was shut.
But in dark of night the child tangled in his sheets
began to brood. Where am I? How did it go:
said Bloodwurst to Liverwurst: 'had I but you . . . '
This only child saw the way the wind would blow,
and mutely understood that he would die, as in the war
had *Dresden, Dresden* . . . lulled defenceless into sleep.

Memory: here's the thing: it starts in certain regions
of the brain and then returns. And origin and home
are just grains of sand in the shifting dunes of neurons.
Blindly, we follow those early paths from childhood on
inscribed into the cortex. And by sense of place we mean:
that this is where it's at, inside your head and not out there:
that's to say what comes and goes in here is *mémoire involontaire*.
Sitting at the bar, it feels like your mind's been
read when Dresden's resurrected from the gutters,
a distant greeting across time and space—from Hypothalamus.

21

OK, that's enough. As for the rest—look to the future:
be like Fröhlich, the Court Fool. Take it as a jest
like the favour of His Majesty, the Golden Rider.
Shit on it, little sparrow on the shoulder of Augustus,
take a moment to enjoy your bird's-eye view
across the patchwork rug of Dresden. It goes down a bomb.
Little thief of crumbs, you know as well as I do
that what this city has endured will one day come
to many more. Each blue spring day we see the birth rate fall.
Ach, that's history . . . why mourn, my cheerful soul?

22

Crazy dream that will not let me be. I am there alone,
unnamed witness to the night of bombs, frozen, mute.
What if you were him, that angel in the skin of stone,
arms spread wide, figure on the cathedral roof?
Below, the city sinks in rubble: he remains unscathed,
hardened by the blaze, ashes cold upon his lips.
Locked inside him, helpless, no one hears you scream.
Are those people popping like chestnuts between
the gutted trams, their charred metal ribs?
Crazy dream: from this cranium nothing escapes.

'No tears for Dresden'

There are things . . . devoted newshound. Is that not so?
Ready for the worst, you always know the score:
the bug-eating plant, the double-headed cow
and the paedophile who quietly sips his beer.
Every shade of monstrous, hot off the press,
with your name on it, comrade—like that piece
yesterday. Lefty students breaking a taboo:
chanting 'Thank you, Harris!' on the anniversary.
Ach, poor bitch, you think, no sense of irony—
as you read about the Dresdener who wants to sue.

Go down again, go down and look inside the air-raid shelter.
Your townsfolk pressed together in their dirty clothes,
fellow Germans, hostage to a mass hysteria,
cursing, sobbing, and beside themselves a moment ago
when the Führer passed by, a Messiah in his Merc,
a national rally for the soul, high day for the Volk.
One great *Sieg Heil* and then a thousand years of shame.
'Davon geht die Welt nicht unter', sang Zarah Leander,
and Radio Satan kept on transmitting just the same.
Just office studs and typing totty still believed in wonders.

'the goose step falters
Odessitka'
Paul Celan, *Threadsuns*

Think of Warsaw, flattened as a prelude: *wiped out*,
when word was: 'Get out, before the Russians come.'
Descendants of those folk, these grim-faced Krauts
whose servitude brought untold splendour to the man
who'd one day reign as King of Poland, Prince of Saxony.
Blitzkrieg, here we go! This band of Uhlan cavalry,
mown down—what chivalry—with tanks. Then the turn:
and *Heim ins Reich* they flee. But first the ghetto *razed*, then
the churches torched; all the roads strewn with mines . . .
At Augustus's Castle the rabble foraged 'til the very end.

How your gentle mother tongue absorbed it all
without a murmur: shrapnel, splinters, shards.
The folksong was the only place to show its gall,
its fear of all the brand-new sparkling verbs.
LTI . . . — shout it and it echoes from the forest dark,
brightly smirking from the shadow of the oak.
And it's: *bulldozed through, blown away, rolled out,*
the gob is mobilized and grabs the megaphones.
Look sharp! Cor Blimey! That's the sound of rats
in their holes, translated into human, just before they croak.

27

'You're asking what that guy is up to, stupid kid,
on the high wire up there with that pole? Holding tight.'
'But father, what will happen if he lets it go?'
Next day in the paper we check to see he got it right.
Don't worry, usually he hovers like he's glued—
perfect balance, while they get dizzy down below.
So says Goethe, 'Although for German there's no rhyme',
in childlike wonder, 'we Germans keep on rhyming all the time.'
The unrhymed one stares perplexed into the void,
listens to the blithe-senseless humming of the word.

Porcelain: from early on the kid was hooked on it.
Like thistledown, this paste for making little punnets,
biscuit porcelain for Brussels lace, edelweiss made solid.
They said this man, this master of *fragilità*, 'shat ducats',
poor sod. But more fool him, imprisoned by the King:
that's what you get, claiming to conjure gold from dirt.
What he found instead was a second crêpe de Chine,
proffered by the earth. Nonetheless, cold comfort.
Like the chiming of a gong that echoes still: terra alba.
A hint of the Far East in the valleys of the Elbe.

How exquisite: snowy white, like Aurora after bathing,
the crockery laid out resplendent on the table.
Coffee, tea and chocolate linger longer on the lips
when you drink from little cups that tinkle as you sip.
Saucers with a rosy sheen, jugs and butter dishes—
Like Cosel's milky neck, the earlobe of Augustus's mistress,
from Kändler's workshop, painted by Eberlein.
All of them besotted by the white-gold porcelain.
Shards bring good luck. But more beautiful by far—
this stoneware-brown, flawless, like the skin of Fatima.

Evening of the wedding party. Cups and saucers, plates
flung by adults to the ground. Unforgettable.
Then the kiss, the happy pair, bride and groom—
A lifetime of love and that begins today.
This moment . . . lost for ever, irrevocable.
Auntie heaves a sigh; though Uncle gives nothing away.
Just a shame about great-grandma's casserole.
What could she do? The turtledoves still need to get a room,
that is: they are 'in love', the wedding snapper thinks, then:
'smile, please' Great God Pan, the good porcelain.

Something shimmers, fine as gossamer, sparkles in the light,
flutters in the muggy Dresden air, tinfoil perhaps?
Come on, think back. The child was all strapped up
ready for a walk, the sky seemed somehow too full, too bright.
Among all the dandelions, balloons and kites, the quiver
as something fell, like steel dust, a metallic glint.
You laughed out loud, in shocked surprise.
Like lametta on the Christmas tree. You had to squint
at its icy glitter. What were these metal slivers?
Was it iron filings danced before your eyes?

'... drawn in cavalier-perspective...'

Old Town on the riverbank, my dearest quarter ... yet
from childhood I've been spellbound by its silhouette.
Close your eyes, then open them again: there, inside
your eyelids you see them, cupolas, towers that stand like
other pines black against the evening sky. Though you're far
away, this heap of stones still seems to draw you in.
A clearing lost in time, in *pittura metafisica*,
as if in its own praise the landscape had sung a hymn.
Taken together here, a city shows itself as the One,
an ensemble, psychotropic, to its late-born son.

Cross-legged like Brahmins, they longed to hover
here, in milder southern climes. The weight of existence
they scorned. Unthinkable, just like the fate of those
Prussian dogs starving daily on the field of honour.
Don't get me started on the Prussians! Enemies of all fine
living, they were peasants, cattle, huddled in their tents.
Ach, even lovely Dresden could not avoid their rigour:
barging in without by nor leave, jack-booted philistines.
The upshot, Europe soon—to paraphrase Voltaire—
looked like the Champs de Mars, a never-ending *cimitière*.

34

The famous plot, late July. . . . Just imagine there
was nothing left of him but a blast-hole in the wall.
Long forgotten too, the whole miserable affair.
Armistice. Dresden standing unscathed still. And all
ends well? No Berlin endgame, no landings at Normandy,
and overnight those spirits that we conjured vanish?
'You ever think what would have happened if?' 'Not me.'
Worse than what we live in now—a world in the subjunctive.
Would have, could have, how they long for a reprieve.
Hans, the dreamer, rubs his eyes and falls asleep.

They say that once a marvel happened in this place.
Floating downstream in the Elbe, on a wooden crucifix,
a blackened Christ and so the good townsfolk fished
him out.—Nothing new in that: wood will always
float. And yet, the pious found their spirits set alight.
The city became a place of pilgrimage. And to this day
Dresden draws its pilgrims in with jewels and gold.
On religion court and nobles went their separate ways,
though, ecumenical and religious, were united
by a sense of beauty that heals all wounds, or so we're told.

36

. . . O George! Those that sat under this mighty dome,
silent in the storm of organ music, can we ever know
what they thought? The Christian, looking down his nose,
found his fellows wanting, as pious folk are wont.
And in the presbytery, we can only guess
what fellow spirit went unrecognized: Sebastian Bach.
In this place such marvels often came to pass.
One brushes past *the other*: Bähr plus Bach and a new world
comes into being. The Art of Fugue, B-Minor Mass.
This task of being human goes on after all. *In-fi-ni-te-si-mal*.

That droning . . . 'Those who lived it never will forget.'
Squadrons in formation rolled across the scene—
Airforce, factory of *Death / Destruction*, hundreds of machines.
Dresden's final hour had tolled: this was it.
Pre-alarms, the main city one, and then, on cue,
His Majesty Fate: white cascades of light:
as though a magnesium flash had lit up the night.
The Greek chorus far below, hey, *masterbomber*,
did you hear it? The people, did they have a clue?
No more search lights. What came next? *Vis major*.

38

'Is that all there is?'

American song

'Thunderclap'. That was it. And in the morning
just a field of rubble left like ancient Troy, Pompeii.
Gog and Magog turned to stone by the Gorgon . . .
Buildings vanished, the damaged falling days
after. No 'how desolate lies the city' from the ruins sounds.
No Aeneas, on his father's back looking to the dawn . . .
For their blindness how wretchedly they atoned.
Five long weeks upon the Altmarkt square, the horses
scratched the straw and watched the griddled corpses
burn. Mawkish? Ach, give over, late-born soul.

Since then, as if her voice had gone, she has been still,
my birthplace on the river: unmoved by distant devotion.
The departing she forgets. And she's had her fill
of mourning weeds. Every last corner so pissed on
by history there's no room left for airs or art.
The composer spoke to her with all his heart
as he recalled the wound of music and fair Lisbon.
Resurrection? Even this she tolerates, though then
sinks back silently resigned, into her old reflection.
Graciously accepts the obituary: *Last Songs*—four of them.

Wait a minute, you don't know the story? Never heard
the tale of mother's vanished doll, its hair of flaxen gold?
Dresden stood in flames and, a tender four-year-old,
Rosi saw her room go up in smoke, her whole world.
Bombed out: a word like that does not sneak up on tiptoes
No, way josé, it arrives in style with 'so it goes'.
Flames as high as houses sucked the air along the streets,
everything ablaze, and all around she heard the screams.
No *nee naa* there to save her. The child, helpless, in the storm,
a little buoy at sea, buffeted by death at every turn.

41

What came of it? Ach, the little doll survived
unscathed, or that is what they say. Hugged to her
breast she held it in her arms, the snoring little mite,
while they sang 'fly ladybird, fly away' for
hours in the cellar. In this circle of very hell,
God be praised, she found herself an aunt as well.
Made no fuss and bravely held her older sister's hand.
Inge was her name, Inge. And this scrap of rags,
looked like it might cry—for the almost-orphan.
Mother in hospital; in farthest Russia father.

Hold on, who's that speaking? Is that crook even Saxon?
Chomping through our yesteryear, the pedant-clown,
cracking jokes, shard-collector, part-time Christian.
What is fate for us, our disgrace—our shame—
is Hecuba for him, Nazi squirt, priggish pioneer,
Never heard the sirens' howl, but cries his tears
all right, not the faintest notion what they are: incendiaries.
The only war they know is on the silver screen, these brats.
Scoffing popcorn in the dark, feet on seats, leant right back,
shadows regurgitating schoolbooks, postwar zombies.

Dearest dead, if you only knew what a child today . . .
But trying to fool the dead is tantamount to hubris.
I'd rather watch the Elbe, trust the *bombing analysts*.
Their facts and figures are way beyond us anyway.
Thirty thousand. Maybe more? A cross upon the map,
that was Dresden, nothing more. Not a place for Job.
Not Sodom, nor Nineveh. According to reports
the dense old housing stock was what made it all go up.
Herr Goebbels claims of history: she is 'a whore'.
And Dresden's downfall? 'Just another trick', she retorts.

44

> 'I was there when Hitler came to power. I was there
> when my Jewish neighbours were taken away. I
> was there when Dresden was destroyed.'
>
> Friedrich Reck

He used to wander there, bored, à la Baudelaire . . .
Postplatz, Altmarkt, Prager Straße, once a boulevard.
They will die like dogs, in concrete. Hard to bear:
such empty space, too much for his naked heart.
This heart sails, you can be sure, until it overflows.
Unshakeably it started to atone for every mess,
all that ever went awry in this place called home.
Day after day . . . too much like therapy and stress.
Those days he thought, odds on I'll survive for sure,
embedded deep within the peace of this Cold War.

Provincial beauty that she was, garrulous, full-bodied.
River like a sash of silver draped around her hips
enticing in the moonlight. But look what they did
to poor Galatea. Is that how to treat the fairer sex?
Swans adorned the dinner service made for Count von Brühl—
flawless just like them you were: proud, curvaceous pin-up girl.
But it almost struck you dumb with shock when the fish,
the shells and dolphins shattered into smithereens,
sinking to the depths where no word could reach.
Who would hide munitions in porcelain tureens?

46

Now watch your step! warns the realist, the inner voice,
those who play with china shards may end up getting hurt.
And does it even cross your mind you've gone too far?
Porcelain: like squinting through a burning glass.
Mirror, mirror . . . let me peek beneath that lacy skirt.
Show me them, the rosebuds . . . lisps the Baroque voyeur.
See the goldfinch peck the bunches of blue grapes
on the little baskets, you can almost hear him sing.
I call on you to witness how things were, dear Harlequin,
Meissen Wonderworld: my solace—*art for its own sake.*

'Filth, dry mixed, softened filth . . .
Spread out stamped on, cleanly severed filth
Painted, glazed, transfigured filth . . . '

Rudolf Borchardt, 'Nomina odiosa'

Not long after Yalta was the moment that it fell.
The old world split in two for the coming fifty years.
Is there such a thing as a wound that cannot heal?
Melancholia . . . Firestorm . . . And the blasted Lares
dancing daily in stilettos on the ever-sorest spot.
So, you see red, son of the city, Don Quixote come-too-late,
one more time you dream the dream of failure:
it's gone, all gone. 'No more baggage—it's for the best',
proclaimed Herr Ley, like other bulls amongst the china.
Что останемся, Stalin? Churchill, Roosevelt, *what's left?*

Martha? Heinrich? It's always you to whom I return.
Kids, the pair of you, first kisses in the thick of war,
until you met that night you'd grown up in uniform.
Heinrich home from the front; Martha in the flak tower.
Rosenkavalier plays softly, trembling you can hardly breathe.
Semper's opera house in darkness, and in the bunker
over his map—and one thing on his mind—the Commander.
Happy end: reserved for Sundays on the silver screen.
This was Tuesday, darkness, *doomsday*. Too late, too far gone
for both of them, White Rose, silver one: the song is done.

49

'No! A bolder bet one cannot lose
than I on the Elbe in those days.'

Goethe, Dresden, 15 August 1813

Come to the centre. Where that lies? Under the stumbling stone
at your feet, deep in the earth.—Wait there, don't go on.
Where dust still whispers, a world in miniature still turns.
Falconers are there, vintners, nymphs with conch-shell horns,
frog-faced putti, figures riding seahorses and swans.
Groups of shepherdesses, lovely gardeners, beasts of lore . . .
Porcelain—most fragile thing. Were these dicey forms
always doomed? What's all this for?—Someone's
listening to hear the daughters of Mnemosyne dictating.
Changing places, times, dimensions as he goes—goes on—creating.

Written between 1992 and 2005

Dresden - Zwinger, Stadtpavillon 8005

Figure 3. The Zwinger Palace, Dresden.

A Glossary

'Porcelain'. Old Italian: 'porcellana', name for a sea snail with a shiny white shell (cowrie shell). From the Latin: 'porcella', piglet or small swine, derived from the Greek 'delphákion' for female pudenda, moist and shiny in a state of arousal.

'Dresden china'. English synonym for porcelain—for products from the Meissen porcelain manufacturer, founded in 1710, the brand with the symbol of the crossed blue swords. Meissen is located on the Elbe, about 25 kilometres downstream from Dresden.

'Por Celan'. The secret formula: give the city over to the poet . . .

Samuel Beckett undertakes a trip through Germany in 1937. The country is on the up and is under the swastika. In Dresden, among other things, he visits the portrait gallery where he meets Will Grohmann, later a Paul Klee specialist, who shows him all the Expressionists in the storage depot, representatives of the so-called 'degenerate art'. In letters to his poet friend Thomas MacGreevy, he speaks of Dresden as the 'porcelain Madonna'.

Virginia Woolf (née Stephen) on the run with her Jewish husband Leonard Sidney Woolf during the Blitz, the German bombing raids on London, which marked the true beginning of city bombardment, years before it returned to its origin and fell on German cities—and finally, contrary to expectation, also on Dresden:

> 'What could we take with us in our little car? Darwin and the silver, some glasses and the porcelain . . .'
>
> (*A Writer's Diary*, 20 October 1940)

Vladimir Nabokov in a short story, during a social evening in New York, among the company a few Germanophile guests:

> 'My Dresden no longer exists', said Mrs Mulberry. 'Our bombs destroyed it and everything it meant.'
>
> (Nabokov, *Conversation Piece*, 1945)

Augustus the Strong (1670–1733), Elector and Duke of Saxony, was crowned King of Poland and Lithuania as Augustus II. His great physical strength earned him the nicknames 'the Strong', 'the Saxon Hercules' and 'Iron-Hand'. It was he who arrested the chemist and alchemist Johann Friedrich Böttger (1682–1719) who had been travelling across the country as a trickster, claiming to have found the 'Philosophers' Stone' and to be able to make gold in his crucibles, and kept him in Königstein Fortress after many failed attempts to make good his claims. Later Augustus brought him to the Albrechtsburg in Meissen, high above the Elbe, where, instead of the promised gold, Böttger produced a malleable white mixture, porcelain, that could be fired in an oven and with which one could make what the Chinese had been making for more than a thousand years: vases, teacups, figurines and all sorts of decorative items that could be painted in a myriad of bright colours. This was the first time that they had become independent of the precious items imported from China, and often paid for in gold, which had dominated East Asian trade for so long. In his desire for Chinese porcelain, Augustus the Strong had once sent 600 Saxon dragoons to the Prussian Soldier King Friedrich Wilhelm I (1688–1740) in exchange for a number of monumental Chinese vases—hence the term 'Dragoon vases'.

The Saxon ruler, who shapes the sensibility of Dresden and its inhabitants to this day, was a lover of the South and the Italian Baroque. As a young man, he had come to know and adore Renaissance and Baroque Italy on his grand tour and already planned an architectural acknowledgement on the banks of the Elbe, the most beautiful Italian city this side of the Alps. 'The desire for porcelain is like the desire for oranges.'

Bruce Chatwin. *Utz* (1988), a novel about the Meissen collector Kaspar von Utz, based on the life story of the Prague porcelain and glass collector Rudolf Just.

> I am not an expert in Meissen porcelain—although my years of traipsing round art museums have taught me what it is. Nor can I say that I like Meissen porcelain. I do, however, admire the boisterous energy of an artist such as Kaendler at play with a

medium which was totally new. And I entirely side with Utz in his feud with Winckel-mann—who, in his 'Notes on the Plebeian Taste in Porcelain' would supplant this plebeian vitality with the dead hand of classical perfection.

I am equally fascinated by the way in which that August's 'porcelain sickness'—the *Porzellankrankheit* of the Augustus the Strong—so warped his vision and that of his ministers, that their delirious schemes for ceramics got mixed up with real political power. Of Brühl, who would become director of the Meissen Manufactory, Horace Walpole commented tartly '. . . he had prepared nothing but baubles against a prince (Frederick the Great) who lived in a camp with the frugality of a common soldier.'

Utz had chosen each item to reflect the moods and facets of the 'porcelain century': the wit, the charm, the gallantry, the love of the exotic, the heartlessness and light-hearted gaiety—before they were sept away by revolution and the tramp of armies.

Czesław Miłosz. Was he the trigger for my porcelain mania? Who can say exactly where the call came from that overtook him? Honestly, his 'Song of Porcelain' (Washington DC, 1947) seems to me to be the initial inspiration. I had his poems (*The Collected Poems, 1931–1987*) bound in leather. 'Sir, Porcelain troubles me most' was the line that pierced my heart. The sad little cry of cups and saucers, cracked, the master's precious dream of roses and shepherds on the meadows had gripped me. Verses on the destruction of these insignificant objects in modern wars, the crunch of broken pieces under the feet of the survivors, you never forget that.

W. H. Auden. Rosetta speaks:
> 'The shops which displayed shining weapons
> And crime-stories carry delicate
> Pastored poems and porcelain groups.'

> ('The Age of Anxiety', Part V, 'The Masque')

Bertolt Brecht, 1944:
> 'And our cities are also just part
> Of all those cities that we destroyed.'

Alfons Paquet:
> 'All cities . . . are tragic. That's why I love them . . . .
> To me, cities are more permanent, more important
> than states.'

> ('Sketch towards a Self-Portrait', 1925)

So much for the approaches. Each line of a poem presupposes hundreds of others, and finally an embrace ensues—in vain? The 'Poem on the Downfall of My City' is a case of impossible troubadour poetry. The city is the lost beloved in the distance.

'Is there a language for the Inferno?' asks Adorno, referring to the hellish agonies of the extermination camps. We know it cannot exist. Even eyewitness accounts cannot account for what really happened. What remains is the interpretation of the trauma: a point at which language must fail. It can only be a question of uncovering the trace of a connection. One can draw a direct line from the German Luftwaffe's first bombing raids against the civilian populations of other countries (Guernica, Warsaw, Rotterdam, London, Belgrade) and the mass murder of the European Jews to the retaliatory attacks against German cities, including, finally, Dresden. The expansion of the inferno zone is the result of German warfare. Collective crimes have paralysed the language and taken away the grief about their own demise.

It is only through the slow processing of the catastrophe in pictures and documents that the buried word becomes visible again. In photography, a $\frac{1}{15}$th of a second exposure time is enough; $\frac{1}{30}$th of a second at most. Imagine a poetics of short exposure times: the need to hold onto the moment in which the word is illuminated in a flash before it sinks back into the twilight of the general language usage.

'Madonna Porcellana' was one of the first keywords written on an index card on the subject. In addition, five handwritten lines, which set the tone (a metrical sketch), but were not used in the final poem.

Drawn back to the precious city time over and again,
Casanova's beauty queen, much the worse for wear.

Poor old dear: you still see glimpses of her better days
on the yellowed pages of the family album. No sanctuary
in the waters of the Elbe. But you can't tear
yourself away. Can't let her, the dementia patient, be.

Notes

1

'Seventeen years'. Since he was born in 1962, seventeen years, a childhood, separates the author from 1945, the end of the war and the year in which the city of his birth was destroyed. 'Siebzehn Jahr blondes Haar', 'Seventeen Years Old, Blond Hair', was a well-known hit by the singer Udo Jürgens (1966).

'Grünbein' means, literally, 'green leg'.

'hiccups'. Doubtless a reference to Paul Celan, the Holocaust poet to whom the cycle is dedicated.

2

'the river's slender S'. The curves of the River Elbe through the Dresden valley form, when seen from a bird's-eye view (the bomber's view), a balanced wavy line like the letter S. According to William Hogarth, this is the so-called 'line of beauty', described in his practical aesthetics *The Analysis of Beauty* (1745).

Figure 4. William Hogarth, 'The Line of Beauty', 1745

'This night is irredeemable.' The first line of a poem by Osip Mandelstam on the death of his mother, August 1916. From the collection *Tristia*.

4

'The Night of Broken Glass'. In the language of the Third Reich, the derisive name for the pogroms on 9 and 10 November 1938, *Reichskristallnacht*, because of all the broken glass. The eyewitness accounts all concur on the shattering and splintering of shop windows, the smashed furniture, glass cabinets, dishes, porcelain; the victims then went through the heaps of their personal belongings. It was the prelude to massive violence against German fellow citizens of the Jewish faith. In the course of a few days, more than 800 Jews were murdered or perished by suicide throughout the German Reich, and hundreds of synagogues were burned. Prayer rooms, cemeteries, apartments and Jewish-owned shops were destroyed indiscriminately (see, above all, Konrad Heiden, *A Night in November 1938: A Contemporary Report*, written in Swiss exile, and published in 1939 in English, Swedish and French).

The bombing of Dresden occurred from Shrove Tuesday to Ash Wednesday 1945. There is a reference to the Narren-sprung (fool's leap), a popular dance jump practised during the Carnival parade.

'German bands'. The last line refers to a speech by Sir Arthur 'Bomber' Harris who led the Allied attacks. When Harris was asked to justify the bombing, following Churchill's famous but subsequently withdrawn memorandum, his reply was succinct:

> The feeling, such as there is, over Dresden could be easily explained by a psychiatrist. It is connected with German bands and Dresden shepherdesses. Actually, Dresden was a mass of munitions works, an intact government centre, and a key transportation centre. It is now none of those things.

5

'Only Germania stands'. Sculpture of Germania, centrally placed at Dresden's Altmarkt, in memory of victory in the Franco-Prussian War of 1870–71. One of many monuments furthering the spirit of nationalism, which appeared everywhere after the founding of the Reich. The Dresden Altmarkt, remarked an eyewitness in 1945: 'Now a pile of rubble.' The stone goddess of the Reich, only slightly damaged, was removed at the end of the 1940s, after the founding of the GDR: Finis Germaniae.

7

The Dresden cherry stone, consisting of 185 carved heads, object of baroque craftsmanship, from the royal art chamber, today the Green Vault collection. They are the heads and faces of sixteenth-century spiritual and secular dignitaries.

8

'The Wreck of the Deutschland'. Ode by Gerard Manley Hopkins (1875/76). The poem deals with the shipwreck of the

Figure 5. Statue of Germania, Altmarkt, Dresden.

Figure 6. Cherry stone with 185 carved heads, Green Vault, Dresden, before 1589.

SS *Deutschland* (North German Lloyd) off the English coast. On board were five Franciscan nuns, whose suffering as émigrées the poet Hopkins lamented in a Jesuit dialogue with God.

'Black snow'. In the 'black snow' we see another reference to Paul Celan's poetry. It refers to the 'black flakes' that are the legacy of the Holocaust. Black snow also appears in Grünbein's poem 'Gedicht uber Dresden' (Poem about Dresden) and the black flakes it suggests appear in 'Europa nach dem letzten Regen' (Europe after the last Rain). See Grünbein's volume *Nach den Satiren*.

'Rubens, Rembrandt, Raphael'. Key painters of the Old Masters Collection. After the invasion of the Red Army, many of the most important paintings were carried off to the Soviet Union as loot, only then to be returned as a cultural gift to the newly founded GDR.

9

'fountain nymph'. The Nymph Fountain, part of the complex built by the Dresden architect Matthäus Daniel Pöppelmann, a key work of local Baroque, created from 1709, the imaginary centre and symbol for the Elbe city.

10

'a bowl of lentil stew'. 'Linseneintopf' presumably referring to biblical story of Esau (Genesis 25:29–34), who swapped his birthright for a mess of pottage. Perhaps also to the 'Eintopfsonntag' (Stew Sunday) instituted throughout the National Socialist Germany in 1933, according to which on the first Sunday of the month only stew was to be eaten and the money saved was to be given to the needy.

'City in the valley'. Allusion to a derogatory name for Dresden, as the most important city in the 'valley of the clueless'. The problem was that Western broadcasting did not penetrate this corner of south-east Germany during the Cold War media campaigns. The Saxons were considered to be the least well-informed people in East Germany.

11

'Hans in Luck'. The hero of the eponymous fairy tale, from *The Children's and Household Tales of the Brothers Grimm*, first published in 1812: a boy whose relentless optimism refuses to countenance reality even as his earnings are taken from him bit by bit.

12

'Florence on the Elbe'. Epithet for Dresden since the beginning of the nineteenth century. Travellers were repeatedly seduced into comparisons by the silhouette of the city.

13

'No sweat, Arthur'. Arthur Travers Harris (1892–1984), popularly known as 'Bomber Harris', Commander-in-Chief of the RAF Bomber Command. The highest authority responsible for air warfare on the British side during the Second World War. His reputation is unjustified: he only carried out what Winston Churchill, as overall commander, ordered. In the end, the airstrikes against German cities, though strategically only following the principle of retaliation, spoke against him; they were certainly always effective. The so-called 'morale' or 'terror bombing' led to complete success. After Germany lost air sovereignty in the bombing war it had itself initiated (Coventry, London, Belfast, etc.), the British-American retaliation appeared to be a singular example of overkill. For the civilian population (and their grandchildren) the Allied air war was so devastating (later, in the GDR it would be known as 'the Anglo-American Terror-Bombing', after a phrase concocted by Goebbels, the Nazi Reich Minister of Propaganda), that the legend of the population's own role as victim came into being. The poem is directed against this. Who would take responsibility for such human disasters? In Western parliamentary debates it turns out: preferably no one.

14

'the seventeenth of April'. The very last bombardment of the city, which had long since been burnt and razed to the ground in a firestorm.

'*Flying Fortress*'. Heavy, so-called horizontal, bomber (Boeing B-17) of the US Air Force, known for its indestructibility, even under the most aggressive enemy fire. A high-flyer sent in to clean up, which quietly finished off the combat zones with its soft roar.

15

'Her subsidence the caesura'. On the morning of 15 February 1945, the Dresden Frauenkirche, badly damaged by the firestorm, collapsed after an improbable fermata. It was as if Johann Sebastian Bach had composed the Requiem for this church building, after a design by George Bähr.

16

'Luther standing there'. Even before the ruins of the Frauenkirche, the destroyed monument of the reformer Martin Luther, badly damaged during the night of the bombing, was erected again (1955). Luther, the Protestant, divider of religions and eloquent anti-Semite, was back, in the midst of the new GDR state founded according to Stalin's specifications. For many years I passed by this bronze monument (which had been inaugurated in 1855 for Reformation Day); I was afraid of the severe expression on his face but did not think anything of seeing him there.

17

'Hogarth's flourish'. Engravings after *The Rake's Progress* by William Hogarth (1697–1764) and other satirical works served as the basis for several plates and figures made by Meissen.

'Venus'. Allusion to the *Sleeping Venus*, a joint work by Giorgione and Titian, along with Raphael's *Sistine Madonna*, one of the key paintings of the Dresden Old Masters' Gallery.

18

'from Hellerau to Cotta'. Districts of Dresden: Hellerau is the remote garden town in the north beyond Hellerberge, until 1989 training ground of the Soviet Army.

'Time to sleep'. In Joseph von Eichendorff, 'Im Abendroth' (At Sunset, 1837), there are the lines: 'The air already darkens' and 'Soon it will be time to sleep'. It was set to music by Richard Strauss as one of the *Four Last Songs* (see Canto 39).

The murderous designs of the **Liverwurst** appear in the peculiar and little-known story 'The Strange Inn' in Grimms' *Household Tales*.

'mémoire involontaire'. French: involuntary memory. Mechanism of spontaneous and individual memory, which goes back to Marcel Proust's novel *À la recherche du temps perdu*, or *In Search of Lost Time* (1913–27). Technique of access to the buried memories of childhood arising from individual sensory impressions.

'Hypothalamus'. Section of the intermediate brain that controls the autonomic functions of the body, the famous 'hormone chamber'.

'Fröhlich, the Court Fool'. Josef Fröhlich was jester at the court of Augustus the Strong (1694–1757). He lived in his own garden house on the banks of the Elbe, the so-called Narrenhäusel. Often depicted in the visual arts of his time. There is a famous bust in Meissen porcelain.

'Golden Rider'. A gilded equestrian statue of Augustus the Strong; one of Dresden's best-known landmarks.

Figure 7. Court Jester Fröhlich (1694–1757), after an etching by Christian Friedrich Boethius of 1729, Kupferstichkabinett, Dresden. Image © Kupferstich-Kabinett, Staatliche Kunstsammlungen Dresden. Photograph by Herbert Boswank.

23

'No tears for Dresden'. Slogan of the left-wing opponents of one-sided commemorations of the victims of the Dresden bombing in the spirit of revanchism.

24

'Zarah Leander'. Swedish actress and singer (1907–81), highest-paid female film star of the Nazi film industry, courted by Goebbels, appreciated by Hitler. Her famous wartime song was 'This Is Not the End of the World'.

25

'Odessitka'. From *Threadsuns* (1968), Celan's last and most extensive volume of poetry. In it is the reference to Odessa and the steps leading down to the harbour, which Sergei Eisenstein made iconic in the film *Battleship Potemkin* (1925). Tsarist soldiers shoot into the crowd and walk in goose step across the corpses. The sequence belongs to the iconography of the Russian Revolution. In her new commentary on Celan's poems (Suhrkamp, 2018), Barbara Wiedemann writes: 'Two women of Odessa (Celan uses the Russian form) are highlighted one after the other in the crowd. The first woman, her injured child in her arms, confronts the soldiers, shouts "Don't shoot!" and is shot nevertheless. The second hurls the pram down the steps when she dies, rolling towards the mounted Cossacks.'

'Think of Warsaw, flattened as a prelude, *wiped out*'. Largest area bombardment against a civilian population in modern times after the attack of the Condor Legion on Guernica,

Figure 8. Odessa Steps (also known at the Primorsky or Potemkin Stairs), Odessa, Ukraine, which famously feature in Sergei Eisenstein's *Battleship Potemkin*.

carried out by the German Luftwaffe in 1939, in the shadow of the Hitler–Stalin Pact. Clear breach of The Hague Land Warfare Convention, which led in turn to each of the further breaches, including the attack against Dresden in the necessary struggle of the Allies against the determination of the German population a few weeks before the expected surrender.

26

'LTI'. *Lingua Tertii Imperii: A Philologist's Notebook* (1947). Victor Klemperer's study of the language in the Third Reich in the form of a diary. Examples from Nazi German include:

aufgerollt (rolled out), *durchgeboxt* (bulldozed through), *abgek-nallt* (blown away), new composites of verbs and preposi-tions, which already revealed everything about the violent character of the regime. The crimes are being prepared for in language.

27

'wire'. The scene on the high wire is from Victor Klemperer's *LTI*.

'The unrhymed one'. Allusion to Celan's poem 'Seelenblind' (from *Threadsuns*) which was written in a psychiatric hospital in Paris. Paraphrase of a line by Osip Mandelstam from 'In Petersburg': 'Seelenblind hinter den Aschen . . . ' (Soulblind, behind the ashes). Celan had begun as a poet of rhyme, keeping alive the memory of his murdered mother, who liked to read poems to him in childhood and loved German rhyme. But outside his early work, the term 'rhyme' appears mostly in negative contexts. It becomes the issue closest to Celan's heart, but also the insoluble conflict at the core of his poetry. Rhyme keeps breaking out right up to the late work.

'Goethe'. From the *Musen-Almanach* of the year 1797, 'Musen und Grazien im Mark' (Muses and Graces in Mark Branden-burg), where it says: 'Though nothing rhymes with German / The German still keeps on rhyming'. It refers to the impos-sibility of finding a rhyme for the word 'German'.

28

'shat ducats'. *Dukatenscheißer* (ducat-shitter) was an insulting epithet for Johann Friedrich Böttger (1682–1719), alchemist and chemist employed at the Dresden court, co-inventor of European hard-paste porcelain.

'terra alba'. So-called white clay or porcelain earth, kaolin, which produces the characteristic white tone in the production of porcelain.

29

'Aurora'. Maria Aurora, Countess of Königsmarck (1662–1728), first mistress of Augustus the Strong. Her great-great-granddaughter was the French writer George Sand.

'Kändler'. Johann Joachim Kändler (1706–75) was the most important modeller of the Meissen porcelain manufacture.

'Cosel's milky neck'. Anna Constantia von Brockdorff, Countess of Cosel (1680–1765), the most famous mistress of Augustus and for a long time the centre of the Saxon court. After an intrigue in which she was involved with the Prussian House of Lords, she was arrested and, in 1716, placed under house arrest at Stolpen Castle for the rest of her life. One of the tragic Saxon figures of legend.

'skin of Fatima'. Maria Aurora von Spiegel, original name Fatima (dates unknown, evidence from 1686–1746), mistress of Augustus, so-called war booty from the wars between the Turkish Empire and the Holy Roman Empire of the German Nation, an unusually attractive woman, companion of Maria Aurora, Countess of Königsmarck.

31

'tinfoil'. Used by the British to disrupt the German short-range radar devices, aluminium or tinfoil strips (also known as Christmas trees) were used as part of an operation code-name 'Window', first deployed in July 1943. The storm of reflected radio signals caused by the strips prevented the aircraft from being accurately located during the attack, leaving the cities defenceless against the bombers.

32

'pittura metafisica'. Italian style of painting, developed in 1917 by Giorgio de Chirico and his brother Alberto Savinio, part of the movement of Futurism.

33

'Voltaire'. Poem about the Lisbon earthquake (1755), the first natural disaster of modern times with thousands of dead—an event that changed everything. A natural event that crystallizes the experience of human impotence in the Enlightenment epoch and serves as proof of God's absence (negative theodicy). At this moment, optimistic belief in progress dies in the European spirit.

The **Champ de Mars** Massacre took place on 17 July 1791 in Paris during the French Revolution.

34

'The famous plot, late July'. The failed attack of 20 July 1944, the last attempt by a group of Wehrmacht officers and conspirators to kill Adolf Hitler and thus to stop the certain demise of the German Reich. Bertolt Brecht, in his *work journal*, 21. 7. 44: 'when snatches of information about the gory goings-on between hitler and the junker generals trickled through, there was a moment where I had my fingers crossed for hitler; for who, if not he, is going to wipe out this band of criminals for us?'

Excursus (draft of a reader's letter after a newspaper review):

> Order must be, and yet: a volume of poems is not an encyclopaedia of world history. What are these verses about? The speaker picks up a figure of thought that is not only widespread, but also pure vernacular. It is the old chestnut of 'what would have been if?' in its misguided German version. This is how it runs: in the event of a successful assassination attempt against Hitler, and the desired cease-fire on the Western Front, would Dresden not have been saved? And with that would not the murder of millions of Jews have been forgotten? At issue here is the larger forgetting by politicians of the right. Forgetting here the terrible deeper meaning of a resetting of German conditions at the expense of all those murdered up to that point, the liquidation of Auschwitz in the name of the 'inner Germany', the musing of Stefan George, which animated Claus von Stauffenberg, the noble knight with the eye patch.

> About the dates: Operation Overlord had begun on 6 June 1944. The period of landings lasted until 29 July. On 20 July, the assassination attempt failed. On 31 July, with the breakthrough of tank units to Avranches, the war of movement in the West began. The most important signals in these verses are the

question marks. It is not asserted but, rather, clothed in a rhetorical question: the poem asks whether what had already—and irrevocably—happened in the real world could have been prevented. And as for the 'intolerable' tone of *Porzellan*: with the rise and fall of each line, these verses are aware of the grief that has never ceased to this day. Through all the facts and files.

36

'O George'. George Bähr (1666–1738), builder of the Dresden Frauenkirche.

38

'Thunderclap'. Operation Thunderclap, official name of the complete destruction that the British RAF Bomber Command planned in order to break the German enemy's will once and for all.

'how desolate lies the city'. This line is taken from the 'Lamentations of Jeremiah' in the Bible. Rudolf Mauersberger (1889–1971), Dresden composer and director of the boys' choir, composed a motet using these verses as part of his 'Dresden cycle', a lament for the destruction of the city in 1945. It is traditionally sung by the Dresdner Kreuzchor before the 'Dresden Requiem'.

39

'*Last Songs*—four of them'. Richard Strauss, *Four Last Songs*, Opus posthumous, after poems by Hermann Hesse and

Joseph von Eichendorff. Death and farewell as a theme, composed in the infamous intoxicating style. Often performed in memory of the demise of Dresden, the city in which the 'God-gifted' Strauss, included at the end of the war in Hitler's so-called 'Important Artists Exempt' list of cultural people worthy of protection, had celebrated some of his greatest successes on stage.

'Today is the happiest day of my life. It's the most beautiful thing I've seen'—Richard Strauss, on visiting Pena Palace, Sintra, just outside Lisbon.

40

'so it goes'. See Kurt Vonnegut's novel *Slaughterhouse-Five, or, The Children's Crusade: A Duty-Dance with Death* (1969). The book that catapulted us directly into the pop era from the Dresden of the GDR era. Less than seven years after my birth, postmodernism had begun in Western literature with the Beatniks.

43

'Herr Goebbels claims of history: she is "a whore"'. Joseph Goebbels (1897–1945), Reich Minister for Propaganda. As Allied victory approaches, the son of a whore notes in the diaries the bitter conclusion that history is a whore.

44

Friedrich Reck-Malleczewen, *Diary of a Man in Despair,* a journal written during the 1930s and '40s in opposition to Hitler and published in 1947.

Although not exterminated, Jews who worked as forced labour in the concentration camps for the German company IG Farben were told that they would **'die like dogs, in concrete'**.

45

'Count von Brühl'. Heinrich Count von Brühl (1700–63), ruler of Electoral Saxony and Polish Prime Minister. Brühl's Terrace in Dresden, the 'balcony of Europe', was named after him. The famous ***Swan Service***, a major work of Meissen porcelain art, which consisted of 2,200 individual pieces— pieces modelled and painted in the Rococo style with aquatic motifs such as swans and water nymphs—was made especially for him: the epitome of the splendour of Saxon Court culture.

47

Rudolf Borchardt's poem cycle *Jamben* (*Iambs*) of 1935–36 is an epode, an all-out attack on the new politics of hatred in Germany. They were written to the backdrop of the Nuremberg Laws, which were declared the same year.

'Not long after Yalta was the moment that it fell'. Conference in the seaside resort of Yalta in the Crimea (4–11 February 1945), at which the Allied heads of state decided on the future division of Germany into a western and eastern sphere of interest.

'Herr Ley'. Robert Ley (1890–1945), Reich leader of the Nazi Party, and leader of the German Labour Front (1933–45). Along with other Nazi leaders, Ley celebrated the destruction of Dresden, the eradication of the 'old civil heritage', as he wrote in the Party newspaper *Der Angriff*: 'This way we march into German victory without the superfluous dead weight and without the heavy ideal and material baggage of bourgeois culture.' He evaded conviction in the trials for major war criminals by committing suicide in his Nuremberg prison cell.

48

'Martha? Heinrich?' Grid reference 'Martha-Heinrich 8'. In radio communications this was German air defence's designation for the Dresden area. Echoes of names of characters from Goethe's *Faust: A Tragedy* (1808). Martha Schwerdtlein and Heinrich Faust?

'White Rose'. Cover name for a resistance group led by students in Munich who, in an anonymous leaflet campaign, called for active opposition to the Hitler regime.

49

'No! A bolder bet one cannot lose'. At the beginning of August 1813, Grand-Duke Karl August invited Goethe to come back to Dresden to see the theatre troupe of the French Court brought there by Napoleon, including the renowned actor Talma. Goethe laid a wager against Councillor Peucer concerning the ceasefire at the time: he bet a ducat on continued peace while Peucer bet on war. A year later Peucer received a letter with a gold ducat and the quoted lines.

Stolperstein or **stumbling stone**. Project initiated by the artist Gunter Demnig in 1992. Small square brass plaques, set into the pavement, are intended to commemorate the fate (deportation, murder or suicide) of people of mainly Jewish descent who were persecuted during the Nazi rule.

'Groups of shepherdesses'. Another reference to Sir Arthur Harris's evaluation of the bombing of Dresden (see note to 4).

'daughters of Mnemosyne'. Mnemosyne, ancient Greek goddess, daughter of Uranos and Gaia, mother of the nine muses.

Visible from far and wide, dancing on the dome of glass,
winged-figure people liked to think of as an angel,
standing on what now is called the lemon press,
though no one here has long since relied on angels.
Fama, that was her: aka Dresden's nemesis,
should she be believed? The gossip girl who spread
what everybody knows today, mixing false and true.
Fama, Fama . . . still gazing down, slender trombonist,
upon the city, screwing your tiny head into the clouds.
You kept well back then, when the blue sky split in two.

(Unpublished)

'lemon press'. Golden figure of the goddess Fama on the glass dome of the Dresden Academy of Fine Arts, Brühl's Terrace. A building by the architect Constantin Lipsius (1832–94).

Translator's Acknowledgements

Thanks are due to the following magazines that have published some of these poems: *Modern Poetry in Translation* and *Raceme*. Individual poems were read on BBC Radio 3 and 4. The translator would also like to thank Michael Eskin for discussions, Iain Galbraith for his careful eye, and all at Seagull Books for their support for this project in the most difficult of circumstances.